Strong Women Have Beliefs and Values

Inspired Words of Wisdom From Strong Women Through the Ages

Adriana Fuentes Díaz

Caliente Press

Strong Women Have Beliefs and Values

Inspired Words of Wisdom from Strong Women Through the Ages

ISBN: 978-1-943702-30-5 (Print edition)
       978-1-943702-31-2 (Kindle edition)

Published by:
Caliente Press
1775 E Palm Canyon Drive, Suite 110-198
Palm Springs, CA 92264
U.S.A.
Email: steven@CalientePress.com

Cover Illustration: Berenice Lacroix
Cover Design: Héctor Castañeda

Endorsements and Praise

I loved the drawings that I found in each category. I fell in love with this and it inspired me to continue reading this wonderful and useful book.

Adriana talks about values and beliefs. She tells us about persistence, freedom, hope, and many others, that I consider have taken higher relevance in the life of women and everybody these days. I found an inspirationally phrase that I would like to share:

> "If I can do it, you can do it. If I can follow my dreams, you can follow your dreams. If I can do this with respect and integrity and morality, you can too." ~ Gina Rodriguez

This phrase is one of many that can be found in this book which inspire and invite us to persevere with our dreams and goals.

Silvia Hernandez P
Marketing & Communication Advisor
England, Venezuela, México

Adriana collects, in eight chosen fundamental values of life, beautiful and inspiring quotes. But when we delve into the reading of each one of them, values and principles of life that draw a roadmap that can lead any woman to live life to the full.

Each passage is a journey to self-exploration of who we are, the awareness of the greatness of women's faculties, the magical sensitivity that is discovered right next to strength, the creative capacity and regenerative nature of our nature, the wisdom of seeing and feeling beyond the palpable, and the unshakable Faith that always appears in women when they face their struggles, lights and processes.

Its reading demands more than simply understanding concepts. *Strong Women Have Beliefs and Values* reminds us of the knowledge we have inside that many are unaware and others have forgotten. But when this knowledge sprouts it becomes the guiding tools for full, dignified and happy lives.

I was grateful to read such a beautiful work, for when reading it brings out smiles, generates peace, draws dreams, reiterates values and principles, and dusts us of distractions about who we really are, raising in our hands the treasure of recognizing our beautiful essence.

Anna Masciarelli Mirás
Lawyer, Marketing and Business Communication
Sustainable Development Specialist
Venezuela

Strong Women Have Beliefs and Values is the second book of a three-part series of *When Strong Women Speak, Strong Women Listen.*

In this edition, Adriana continues to explore the thoughts and beliefs of legendary women across the world. It is truly grounding to see how each and every one of these women faced adversities throughout their lives, just like the rest of us, and yet remained courageous at heart.

It is easy to read and the ideal night table book. Each page shows the beauty in life. It will put a smile on your face and motivate you to keep dreaming.

Vanessa Alvarez
Woman, wife, daughter, friend
Marketing Specialist
Canada

I'm in love with this book. Each chapter forced me to follow the next one. A wonderful reading with beautiful paintings.

I was touched. *Strong Women Have Beliefs and Values* inspired me, gave me strength, gave me *Berraquera* as they say in my native Colombia. It is a perfect read to fill us with the energy to face great, and not so great, moments in life. It is wonderful book to fill us with love and solidarity.

Now is the time, women, to understand that if we support each other, it will be easier to attain our dreams and goals. This life is to share it and to prosper as a team. Adri, I congratulate you.

Carol Montealegre Cárdenas
Director, Idear Eventos
México

This book should be read by everyone that want to reconnect and motivate themselves at any time. The topics of the quotes Adriana chose for this book really make you believe that impossible is nothing and determination is the key to succeed.

Patricia Medina
Marketing Manager
Venezuela

Contents

Dedication

I dedicate this book to you Steven.

Since we started this wonderful Strong Women Speak trilogy project together a year ago, these three books went from being a dream to a tangible and beautiful reality.

Without your dedication, enthusiasm, guidance, and support, these books would not have been possible.

I thank you for every hour that you invested in each one, for your work on them during weekends, early mornings, and some nights until late. For being flexible with me in delivery times and for having had so much patience when something did not turn out as you expected.

I am convinced that the results this project has brought us both were worth it.

Personally, having launched this beautiful trilogy, I now feel a happier, fuller, more human, more sensitive woman, more committed to other women and finally, more united to you.

Thank you are wonderful!

Adriana Fuentes Díaz

Elegance isn't defined by what you wear.
It's how you carry yourself,
how you speak, what you read!

Carolina Herrera

Introduction

I opened this book with one of my favorite Carolina Herrera quotes, for she has inspired me throughout my life. Her quote has continuously reminded me that I can fly over any hurdle, obstacle, difficulty, or challenge that life throws at me.

This book is the second in a beautiful trilogy, focused on giving all women the motivation, courage, strength, and inspiration to achieve all their dreams.

At different stages of my life, many women of different nationalities, professions, ages, cultures, races, and education have given me the necessary motivation, courage, and strength to keep going through their wise words and strong examples.

As I think back over recent history, I realize the difficult roles and challenges that women have had, both personally and professionally, to help us women gain our rightful place in society. I admire and value these strong women and what our gender has achieved. From being able to vote, to how to decide for our own professional and personal futures are great steps in which we should all feel proud.

Because of the progressive actions of women in developed countries to access formal education, we have gained a fundamental platform that provided them with a very powerful weapon of training and information, through which we have channeled our aspirations, desires for social improvement, and political demands. There is no doubt that education, training, and access to information has also helped women integrate and, to an extent, advance in many labor markets as well.

However, despite the advances we have made in the more developed countries of the world, there is still much to do and work to leave to the new generations of girls a world with greater equity and inclusion, less gender violence, and greater participation and leadership in all aspects of society.

Surely it will not be an easy task either, but when we sow the best fruits, we will obtain the best harvests. All generations of young women must be supported, motivated, and encouraged to pursue their dreams and goals; since there is nothing impossible in life that cannot be achieved with discipline, perseverance, and inspiration.

I also believe that it is time to proactively help each other, to be more solidary, united, and to support each other more. We need to be uncompetitive with one another. And, above all, we need to learn to respect ourselves as women and human beings.

I am who I am today, because each person who has entered my life has touched it in a different and special way. I am grateful for the wonderful people I have had at my side in this journey that is life. The blows, learning, and experiences are part of it and make us learn to be more humble, honest, loving, and better human beings.

My Friendship with Berenice

One such person who has touched me deeply is Berenice, the artist whose drawings in this book and on the cover provide an additional dimension. Our friendship started eight years ago, when we met at our children's school.

While we share school activities with the children, we got to know each other better and realized the great affinity we have on so many relevant topics in our lives. Our friendship grew and strengthened, as well as my great admiration for her painting.

Berenice is a dedicated, committed, fun, and very versatile artist. When I told Berenice about the nature of this beautiful trilogy, she immediately identified with this project. Mixing her painting style and my writing, she has captured on canvas the different stages and moments that women live during our journeys through life.

We shared many afternoons together talking about the values and beliefs that are the foundation of the *When Strong Women Speak* series of books. While Berenice painted, we discussed the importance of these values and beliefs and how they impact our thinking and actions. Sometimes a delicious coffee and porridge accompanied us, and at other times an exquisite wine complemented by Berenice's Chiapas cuisine!

Throughout our many discussions on developing these three books, there has been a perfect synchronicity and understanding between us. Not surprisingly, our friendship grew strong and reinforced by belief on how important it is to help and support one another. Plus, everything is easier and more fun when you share your passion with a great friend!

As author Louise Berniknow wrote, "Female friendships that work are relationships in which women help each other belong to themselves."

Be Inspired

In this second book you will find beautiful illustrations that Berenice painted, inspired by personal meaning for each category. You will also read what each of these categories means to me, from the bottom of my heart. I hope you enjoy this book as much as I do and, above all, it inspires you in everything you set out to do in life.

In this book I will write about the values that give life meaning. Human values are what demonstrate the kind of person we are. Some of these values are courage, hope, persistence, freedom, passion, and others that I consider extremely important. The world in which we live today unfortunately suffers more and more every day from a lack of these values, as too many people seem to place greater importance on selfishness, personal interests, and indifference towards others.

For my personal and professional goals, I have always sought to stay inspired to achieve each of my projects. Today, I now want to inspire, with this book and my future endeavors, many more women around the world.

Finally, I hope I have made this book an excellent gift for your mother, daughter, best friend, sister, cousin, or colleague. My idea is that *When Strong Women Speak, Strong Women Listen* will serve as inspiration for many women in your life and for the next generations of women who will surely have an increasingly important and leading role in this world.

Adriana Fuentes Díaz
February 2021

My Story

I was born in Mexico City, but I grew up in Venezuela, a place in which I was happy for 35 years. Its climate, people, and the beauty of its land gave me the best years of my life. I also lived in Newark, Delaware, and Montreal.

I had the opportunity to work in two excellent multinational companies, HBO (Sony Entertainment TV) and BBDO. In both, I learned, traveled, and grew a lot as a professional. I was surrounded by incredible people, who were very capable, professional, and humane.

After the very fast, sad, and depressing deterioration in Venezuela, I decided to start a new life. I left Caracas at the age of 38 with four suitcases, my son, and my beautiful dog Cala to return to Mexico City. I journeyed into an unknown adventure, where I carried with me only my good attitude, faith, and a belief in myself and my potential as both a woman and a professional, combined with the desire for success as my main tools. Some members of my family did not agree with that decision, but the most important thing at the time was I believed in myself.

A few years later, as I look back and remember that moment as if it had been yesterday, I realize how strong and determined women can be when we pursue our dreams. Sometimes, we do not value ourselves in the face of many difficult circumstances that happen in our lives. But, it is in these situations, that we need a little more belief and appreciation for "our-self."

Now, with 15 years of experience in several companies in the corporate world, in both national and regional positions, I am reinventing myself and focusing on what I am really passionate about. This includes writing, traveling, helping the most helpless people and animals, and the field of decoration and details. I now realize life is too short to waste on dedicating ourselves to anything that does not make us happy.

Almost a year ago, I launched my decoration blog (www.decoracionyalgomas.com) where week after week I give ideas and tips on how to decorate the different spaces of your house, office, or garden with a low budget and original and different details.

Finally, I feel very fortunate in each and every one of the personal and professional experiences I have had in my life. Thanks to each one of them, I have learned to be braver, stronger, persistent, optimistic, happy, and to fight tirelessly for my dreams.

I hope you enjoy this book as much as I do and, above all, it inspires you in everything you do and set out in life. My very best wishes to you.

CHAPTER 1

Persistence

I hesitate between persistence and foolishness. I hesitate between the two. Knowing the result gives me the distance and this happens when I look back and observe what has been created, thus discovering the constant work as something wonderful or as something that got out of hand.

Artist

Persistence takes us to that next level where we want to be better, where we are sure we can give better results. Those who never give up are persistent despite the stones that cross our paths and before the falls that make us stronger. It is the art of standing firm and still, before acting, that result in making the best decisions for ourselves.

Author

Persistence Quotes

I had to work extra hard. It's not easy for Latinos to get education, but I'm trying to make a difference. I dreamed of being at the top, and I'm not going to give up.
Abigail Rodriguez

At the end of the day, we can endure much more than we think we can.
Frida Kahlo

Sometimes a breakdown can be the beginning of a kind of breakthrough, a way of living in advance through a trauma that prepares you for a future of radical transformation.
Cherrie Moraga

If you know you are on the right track, if you have this inner knowledge, then nobody can turn you off...no matter what they say.
Barbara McClintock

You can often change your circumstances by changing your attitude.
Eleanor Roosevelt

Nothing has transformed my life more than realizing that it's a waste of time to evaluate my worthiness by weighing the reaction of the people in the stands.
Brené Brown

As my mom always said growing up, "When you do something, do it *con ganas*." To her, that phrase extended to the way in which my siblings and I not only pursued our careers, but to how neatly we swept the floor. So, whether you're early in your career and have to side hustle as a barista, or have finally made your way to the corner office — do it all *con ganas*.
Analisa Cantu

You can't control things; you can only postpone the inevitable.
Danielle Joseph

A stumbling block to the pessimist is a stepping-stone to the optimist.
Eleanor Roosevelt

Sometimes, no matter how much people care about you, they will not always understand or support your vision—and that is perfectly okay. It is yours for a reason, so dare to swim against the current in pursuit of whatever it is you dream of. In the end, you will find there is no greater success than achieving what you believe in and make happen on your own.
Anixia Rodriguez

I just love bossy women. I could be around them all day. To me, bossy is not a pejorative term at all. It means somebody is passionate and engaged and ambitious and doesn't mind learning.
Amy Poehler

If I fail to follow my morning routine, I try to get a hard workout in. A hard workout is like a manual restart of the day.
Aubrey Marcus

I really built myself up, darn it, to be very strong.
Barbara Bush

I have learned over the years that when one's mind is made up, this diminishes fear.
Rosa Parks

You may be disappointed if you fail, but you are doomed if you don't try.
Beverly Sills

You must do the thing you think you cannot do.
Eleanor Roosevelt

Brave doesn't mean you're not scared. It means you go on even though you're scared.
Angie Thomas

You deserve the best, the very best, because you are one of the few people in this lousy world who are honest to themselves, and that is the only thing that really counts.
Frida Kahlo

Look at me. I came from nothing. I'm using my voice. I don't know where it's going to take me. But I've got you listening. You can do the same.
Diane Guerrero

Getting stress out of your life takes more than prayer alone. You must take action to make changes and stop doing whatever is causing the stress. You can learn to calm down in the way you handle things.
Joyce Meyer

Do not let your mind bully your body into believing it must carry the burden of its worries.
Astrid Alauda

Do the things that interest you and do them with all your heart. Don't be concerned about whether people are watching you or criticizing you. The chances are, they aren't paying attention to you.
Eleanor Roosevelt

Generally, by the time you are Real, most of your hair has been loved off, and your eyes drop out and you get loose in the joints and very shabby. But these things don't matter at all, because once you are Real you can't be ugly, except to people who don't understand.
Margery Williams

Beliefs and values are choices. When our beliefs and values evolve, so do we.
Marilyn Monroe

Whatever is being experienced, just allow it and let it be.
Elisha Goldstein

Look for a way to lift someone up. And if that's all you do, that's enough.
Elizabeth Lesser

Slow down, you'll get there faster.
Katherine King

When you take risks, you learn that there will be times when you succeed and there will be times when you fail, and both are equally important.
Ellen DeGeneres

Sometimes the most important thing in a whole day is the rest we take between two deep breaths.
Etty Hillesum

Can verbs be made up? I'll tell you one. I heaven you, so my wings will open wide to love you boundlessly. I am not sick. I am broken. But I am happy to be alive as long as I can paint.
Frida Kahlo

Your absence has gone through me like thread through a needle. Everything I do is stitched with its color.
W. S. Merwin

Although there is much to be sad about, there is also much to be celebrated. You are watching what is a pivotal moment in this country's evolution.
Lady Gaga

Just because we didn't measure up to some standard of achievement doesn't mean that we don't possess gifts and talents that only we can bring to the world. Just because someone failed to see the value in what we can create or achieve doesn't change its worth or ours.
Brené Brown

I am convinced that every effort must be made in childhood to teach the young to use their own minds. For one thing is sure: If they don't make up their minds, someone will do it for them.
Eleanor Roosevelt

Actually, spending ten minutes clearing off one shelf is better than fantasizing about spending a weekend cleaning out the basement.
Gretchen Rubin

If I can do it, you can do it. If I can follow my dreams, you can follow your dreams. If I can do this with respect and integrity and morality, you can too.
Gina Rodriguez

A man does what he can; a woman does what a man cannot.
Isabel Allende

I think that little by little I'll be able to solve my problems and survive.
Frida Kahlo

Between saying and doing, many a pair of shoes is worn out.
Iris Murdoch

Forget about what you have to do for a second. How do you want to be for today?
Jane Scudder

We do not have to become heroes overnight. Just a step at a time, meeting each thing that comes up, seeing it as not as dreadful as it appears, discovering that we have the strength to stare it down.
Eleanor Roosevelt

Doubt is a killer. You just have to know who you are and what you stand for.
Jennifer Lopez

Being perfect is being flawed, accepting it, and never letting it make you fell less than you best.
Jessica Alba

If you look confident you can pull off anything – even if you have no clue what you're doing.
Jessica Alba

It does not do to dwell on dreams and forget to live.
J.K. Rowling

Never give up. Always find a reason to keep trying.
Kelly Mizell

For fast-acting relief, try slowing down.
Lily Tomlin

You can be whatever you want to be. Just be honest and kind. And be the kind of person who helps other people see their worth and beauty.
Lori Deschene

Mindfulness is like taking your brain for a virtual walk. Like our bodies, our minds need time to recover after a difficult workout. It is a way to 'walk' it off—catch your breath, settle your muscles, and be fully present. Notice what you see, smell, feel, and hear. Be in the moment as you gain insight and nurture yourself. Even a few seconds or minutes is enough. Don't overthink—it isn't the formal practice of meditation ... and you don't need sneakers.
Lori Maney Lentini

The thing that makes you exceptional, if you are at all, is inevitably that which must also make you lonely.
Lorraine Hansberry

Ego says "Once everything falls into place, I'll find peace." Spirit says "Find your peace and then everything will fall into place."
Marianne Williamson

Success must include two things: the development of an individual to his utmost potentiality and a contribution of some kind to one's world.
Eleanor Roosevelt

I am in agreement with everything my father taught me and nothing my mother taught me.
Frida Kahlo

Being in control of your life and having realistic expectations about your day-to-day challenges are the keys to stress management, which is perhaps the most important ingredient to living a happy, healthy and rewarding life.
Marilu Henner

Your ambition should be to get as much life out of living as you possibly can, as much enjoyment, as much interest, as much experience, as much understanding. Not simply be what is generally called a 'success.
Eleanor Roosevelt

The progress of the world will call for the best that all of us have to give.
Mary McLeod Bethune

This is your time and it feels normal to you but really there is no normal. There's only change, and resistance to it and then more change.
Meryl Streep

I am a woman, a socialist, separated and agnostic — all the sins together.
Michelle Bachelet

You know you've reached middle age when you're cautioned to slow down by your doctor, instead of by the police.
Joan Rivers

What you don't do can be a destructive force.
Eleanor Roosevelt

You have to be doing things that matter. Responsibility, but also responsibility with epic and beautiful and noble tasks.
Michelle Bachelet

I am that clumsy human, always loving, loving, loving. And loving. And never leaving.
Frida Kahlo

Being defeated is often a temporary condition. Giving up is what makes it permanent.
Marilyn Vos Savant

I find that when you have a real interest in life and a curious life, that sleep is not the most important thing.
Martha Stewart

Stress is an ignorant state. It believes that everything is an emergency.
Natalie Goldberg

Mindfulness is a simple practice, but not an easy one … but you are worth doing hard things.
Nicole Davis

The most important part of the body is the brain. Of my face, I like the eyebrows and eyes.
Frida Kahlo

Above all, don't fear difficult moments. The best comes from them.
Rita Levi-Montalcini

The reward for conformity is that everyone likes you but yourself.
Rita Mae Brown

It takes as much energy to wish as it does to plan.
Eleanor Roosevelt

If you're not making some notable mistakes along the way, you're certainly not taking enough business and career chances.
Sallie Krawcheck

Words fall short whenever I want to tell you how special you are to me, but all I can say is, that my world is full of smiles whenever I think of you.
Natalie Anderson

Whatever we are waiting for—peace of mind, contentment, grace, the inner awareness of simple abundance—it will surely come to us, but only when we are ready to receive it with an open and grateful heart.
Sarah Ban Breathnach

When wealth is passed off as merit, bad luck is seen as bad character. This is how ideologues justify punishing the sick and the poor. But poverty is neither a crime nor a character flaw. Stigmatize those who let people die, not those who struggle to live.
Sarah Kendzior

If you are broken, you do not have to stay broken.
Selena Gomez

They thought I was surrealist, but I wasn't. I never painted dreams. I painted my own reality.
Frida Kahlo

Mindfulness isn't difficult. We just have to remember to do it.
Sharon Salzberg

My brain, I believe, is the most beautiful part of my body.
Shakira

Forgiveness isn't just the absence of anger. I think it's also the presence of self-love, when you actually begin to value yourself.
Tara Westover

The purpose of life is to live it, to taste experience to the utmost, to reach out eagerly and without fear for newer and richer experience.
Eleanor Roosevelt

You don't get over it, you just get through it. You don't get by it, because you can't get around it. It doesn't 'get better'; it just gets different. Everyday grief puts on a new face.
Wendy Feireisen

CHAPTER 2

Passion

The imprint in which I live developing myself in the works feels cathartic and repetitive. Trying to contain the feeling, the ever-present passion, makes a new and different meeting of the same song thanks to those silences and those wild screams that enter at different times.

Artist

Life itself, writing, reading, animals, travel, exercise, my family, my friends are my passions. I cannot conceive of my life without doing or dedicating myself to what I am passionate about. It is a feeling that dominates my will. It is an emotion that runs through my veins before something or someone.

Passion produces an absolute satisfaction that is felt in all of us. Passion for something means always wanting to repeat it. It is feeling an indescribable degree of happiness and pleasure in doing what you are doing.

Author

Passion Quotes

You are magnificent beyond measure, perfect in your imperfections, and wonderfully made.
Abiola Abrams

Do what you feel in your heart to be right – for you'll be criticized anyway.
Eleanor Roosevelt

Do something nice for yourself today. Find some quiet, sit in stillness, breathe. Put your problems on pause. You deserve a break.
Akiroq Brost

As my knowledge of things grew I felt more and more the delight of the world I was in.
Helen Keller

"Thank you" is the best prayer that anyone could say.
Alice Walker

Nothing is absolute. Everything changes, everything moves, everything revolves, everything flies and goes away.
Frida Kahlo

The way you tell your story to yourself matters.
Amy Cuddy

Carve out and claim the time to care for yourself and kindle your own fire.
Amy Ippoliti

So, here I am, all by myself, thinking of you – no one else. There's a feeling inside and as hard as I try, it just won't go away.
Angel Hema

How wonderful it is that nobody needs to wait a single moment before starting to improve the world.
Anne Frank

Self-care means considering yourself a worthwhile person and presenting yourself as valuable, capable, and deserving. In other words, self-care seeks to redress an imbalance that develops when you don't take proper care of yourself, whether by inattention or by choice.
Arin Murphy-Hiscock

Compassionate people ask for what they need. They say no when they need to, and when they say yes, they mean it. They're compassionate because their boundaries keep them out of resentment.
Brené Brown

Life is a succession of lessons which must be lived to be understood.
Helen Keller

Only I can change my life. No one can do it for me.
Carol Burnett

All of life is a constant education.
Eleanor Roosevelt

Front-loading my day (getting a whole bunch done in the morning) is my productivity secret.
Celeste Headlee

There is no way that i could being to explain to someone what it feels like being without you. I would say it's like the earth without the sky.
Cindy Adkins

Beauty begins the moment you decide to be yourself.
Coco Chanel

Painting completed my life. I lost three children and a series of other things that would have fulfilled my horrible life. My painting took the place of all of this. I think work is the best.
Frida Kahlo

I love a warm bath at the end of a day.
Cynthia Nixon

There is only one page left to write on. I will fill it with words of only one syllable. I love. I have loved. I will love.
Dodie Smith

It is not more vacation we need – it is more vocation.
Eleanor Roosevelt

Life is very interesting... in the end, some of your greatest pains, become your greatest strengths.
Drew Barrymore

Had I not loved so much I would not hurt so much. I will hurt. And I will be grateful for that hurt for it bears witness to the depth of our meaning. And for that I will be eternally grateful.
Dr. Elisabeth Kubler-Ross

There are two ways of spreading light: to be the candle or the mirror that reflects it.
Edith Wharton

I paint flowers so they will not die.
Frida Kahlo

I could not at any age be content to take my place in a corner by the fireside and simply look on.
Eleanor Roosevelt

Vulnerability is not knowing victory or defeat; it's understanding the necessity of both; it's engaging. It's being all in.
Brené Brown

One's philosophy is not best expressed in words; it is expressed in the choices one makes...and the choices we make are ultimately our responsibility.
Eleanor Roosevelt

Do whatever brings you to life, then. Follow your own fascinations, obsessions, and compulsions. Trust them. Create whatever causes a revolution in your heart.
Elizabeth Gilbert

Whatever our souls are made of, his and mine are the same.
Emily Brontë

You're only human. You live once and life is wonderful, so eat the damned red velvet cupcake.
Emma Stone

Whatever you do, do it with passion. The rest comes by itself.
Fabiola Haro

My mother always says people should be able to take care of themselves, even if they're rich and important.
Frances Hodgson Burnett

It is never too late to be what you might have been.
George Eliot

The only thing you can do in this life is to pursue your passions, celebrate your bloopers and never stop following your fear.
Grace Helbig

Life is what we make it, always has been, always will be.
Grandma Moses

The beautiful spring came; and when Nature resumes her loveliness, the human soul is apt to revive also.
Harriett Ann Jacobs

Enjoy every minute you have with those you love, my dear, for no one can take joy that is past away from you. It will be there in your heart to live on when the dark days come.
Eleanor Roosevelt

When we do the best we can, we never know what miracle is wrought in our life or the life of another.
Helen Keller

I want to be inside your darkest everything.
Frida Kahlo

I wish, as well as everybody else, to be perfectly happy; but, like everybody else, it must be in my own way.
Jane Austen

It's never too late – never too late to start over, never too late to be happy.
Jane Fonda

I love you more than my own skin.
Frida Kahlo

There are no regrets in life, just lessons.
Jennifer Aniston

To be mature you have to realize what you value most... Not to arrive at a clear understanding of one's own values is a tragic waste. You have missed the whole point of what life is for.
Eleanor Roosevelt

Before I leave the house, I say five things I love about myself, like 'You have really pretty eyes.' That way I can go out into the world with that little bit of extra confidence.
Jennifer Love Hewitt

I enjoy life when things are happening. I don't care if it's good things or bad things. That means you're alive.
Joan Rivers

A mother's grief is as timeless as her love.
Joanne Cacciatore

Sorrow is so easy to express and yet so hard to tell.
Joni Mitchell

I am my own muse. I am the subject I know best. The subject I want to better.
Frida Kahlo

The voice of the sea is seductive, never ceasing, whispering, clamoring, murmuring, inviting the soul to wander in abysses of solitude.
Kate Chopin

I think that somehow, we learn who we really are and then live with that decision.
Eleanor Roosevelt

Life is short, and it is here to be lived.
Kate Winslet

You don't have to think about love; you either feel it or you don't.
Laura Esquivel

A good book gives us insight into its characters; a great book gives us insight into ourselves.
Lydia Perovic

Never be bored, and you will never be boring.
Eleanor Roosevelt

The true birthplace is that wherein for the first time one looks intelligently upon oneself; my first homelands have been books, and to a lesser degree schools.
Marguerite Yourcenar

Love is holy because it is like grace – the worthiness of its object is never really what matters.
Marilynne Robinson

Every day brings new choices.
Martha Beck

Keep smiling, because life is a beautiful thing and there's so much to smile about.
Marilyn Monroe

My mission in life is not merely to survive, but to thrive; and to do so with some passion, some compassion, some humor, and some style.
Maya Angelou

Don't give it five minutes if you're not going to give it five years.
Meghan Markle

Self-care is your fuel ... Whatever the road ahead or the path you've taken, self-care is what keeps your motor running and your wheels turning.
Melissa Steginus

I want to feel my life while I'm in it.
Meryl Streep

I leave you my portrait so that you will have my presence all the days and nights that I am away from you.
Frida Kahlo

Spread love everywhere you go. Let no one ever come to you without leaving happier.
Mother Teresa

People's souls are like gardens. You can't turn your back on someone because his garden's full of weeds. You have to give him water and lots of sunshine.
Nancy Farmer

Above all, be the heroine of your life, not the victim.
Nora Ephron

We're all capable of climbing so much higher than we usually permit ourselves to suppose.
Octavia E. Butler

So, I say to you, forget about the fast lane. If you really want to fly, just harness your power to your passion. Honor your calling. Everybody has one. Trust your heart and success will come to you.
Oprah Winfrey

You cannot make yourself feel something you do not feel, but you can make yourself do right in spite of your feelings.
Pearl S. Buck

A smile is a curve that sets everything straight.
Phyllis Diller

Every one of us needs to show how much we care for each other and, in the process, care for ourselves.
Princess Diana

If life were predictable it would cease to be life, and be without flavor.
Eleanor Roosevelt

Grief is the price we pay for love.
Queen Elizabeth II

Know this one great truth: you are in control of your own life.
Rachel Hollis

I saw two fallen branches in the shape of a heart. Thought of you.
Stephanie Perkins

Late at night when all the world is sleeping, I stay up and think of you. And I wish on a star that somewhere you are thinking of me too.
Selena Quintanilla Perez

You can waste your lives drawing lines. Or you can live your life crossing them.
Shonda Rhimes

I used to love night best but the older I get the more treasures and hope and joy I find in mornings.
Terri Guillemets

Happiness is a choice. You can choose to be happy. There's going to be stress in life, but it's your choice whether you let it affect you or not.
Valerie Bertinelli

Life isn't about waiting for the storm to pass; it's about learning to dance in the rain.
Vivian Greene

Take a lover who looks at you like maybe you are a bourbon biscuit.
Frida Kahlo

There are some things you learn best in calm, and some in storm.
Willa Cather

Smile in the mirror. Do that every morning and you'll start to see a big difference in your life.
Yoko Ono

Tomorrow is a mystery. Today is a gift. That is why it is called the present.
Eleanor Roosevelt

Turn your wounds into wisdom.
Oprah Winfrey

CHAPTER 3

Hope

In my painting hope is necessary. A change causes a delight to pass from a moment of peace to another that throws you into change. The simple fact of being what I am and being better is the very hope that walks when I paint and within what I paint.

Artist

Hope gives us the confidence to achieve everything we want and desire in life. It is an optimistic state of mind, which helps us understand that what we aspire to seems viable or possible. It is a virtue that helps us achieve everything we want or dream of.

As is often said, "hope is the last thing that is lost."

Author

Quotes on Hope

In the long run, the sharpest weapon of all is a kind and gentle spirit.
Anne Frank

One can never pay in gratitude; one can only pay 'in kind' somewhere else in life.
Anne Morrow Lindbergh

The giving of love is an education in itself.
Eleanor Roosevelt

Then you must teach my daughter this same lesson. How to lose your innocence but not your hope. How to laugh forever.
Amy Tan

The more you praise and celebrate your life, the more there is in life to celebrate.
Oprah Winfrey

Strive to find things to be thankful for, and just look for the good in who you are.
Bethany Hamilton

You have dug your soul out of the dark, you have fought to be here; do not go back to what buried you.
Bianca Sparacino

I would hope that a wise Latina woman with the richness of her experiences would more often than not reach a better conclusion than a white male who hasn't lived that life.
Sonia Sotomayor

Before you conquer the mountain, you must learn to overcome your fear.
Isabel Allende

The culture of shame is driven by fear, blame and disconnection, and it is often a powerful incubator for issues like perfectionism, stereotyping, gossiping and addiction.
Brené Brown

Nothing is worth more than laughter. It is strength to laugh and to abandon oneself, no be light. Tragedy is the most ridiculous thing.
Frida Kahlo

We must be impatient for change. Let us remember that our voice is a precious gift and we must use it.
Claudia Flores

Listen to God with a broken heart. He is not only the doctor who mends it but also the father who wipes away the tears.
Criss Jami

What I didn't understand—what I suddenly realize now—was that if I stopped moving backwards, trying to recapture the past, there might be a future waiting for me, waiting for us, a future that would reveal itself if only I turned around and looked, and that once I did, I could start to move toward it.
Cristina Henriquez

Waking up early, connecting with nature, and having my quiet time are priorities to me, and they are non-negotiable.
Danette May

If I need to remind myself to bring something with me in the morning, I'll usually put my car keys on top of it.
Des Traynor

I hope the fathers and mothers of little girls will look at them and say "yes, women can."
Dilma Rousseff

The way I see it, if you want the rainbow, you gotta put up with the rain.
Dolly Parton

There are two ways of spreading light: to be the candle or the mirror that reflects it.
Edith Wharton

If you really listen to someone – put yourself in their shoes and pay attention to what they're saying and who they are with as little judgment as you can manage – the results are always better.
Eileen Fisher

Character building begins in our infancy and continues until death.
Eleanor Roosevelt

Just because someone isn't willing or able to love us, it doesn't mean that we are unlovable.
Brené Brown

It seems to me of great importance to teach children respect for life.
Eleanor Roosevelt

People grow through experience if they meet life honestly and courageously.
Eleanor Roosevelt

Well, I hope that if you are out there and read this and know that, yes, it's true I'm here, and I'm just as strange as you.
Frida Kahlo

We are afraid to care too much, for fear that the other person does not care at all.
Eleanor Roosevelt

No life is so hard that you can't make it easier by the way you take it.
Ellen Glasgow

Given another shot at life, I would seize every minute of it ... look at it and really see it ... try it on ... live it ... exhaust it ... and never give that minute back until there was nothing left of it.
Erma Bombeck

We are always going to have prejudices. I don't think we can change society. You can only change individual by individual. And you can change yourself.
Esmeralda Santiago

Justice cannot be for one side alone, but must be for both.
Eleanor Roosevelt

The tragedy in the lives of most of us is that we go through life walking down a high-walled lane with people of our own kind, the same economic situation, the same national background and education and religious outlook. And beyond those walls, all humanity lies, unknown and unseen, and untouched by our restricted and impoverished lives.
Florence Luscomb

Love beauty, it is the shadow of God on the universe.
Gabriela Mistral

Silent gratitude isn't very much to anyone.
Gertrude Stein

Every time you meet a situation you think at the time it is an impossibility and you go through the tortures of the damned, once you have met it and lived through it, you find that forever after you are freer than you were before.
Eleanor Roosevelt

Every morning, my dad would have me looking in the mirror and repeat: "Today is going to be a great day; I can, and I will.
Gina Rodriguez

Life is what we make it, always has been, always will be.
Grandma Moses

Avoiding danger is no safer in the long run than outright exposure. The fearful are caught as often as the bold.
Helen Keller

I would hope that a wise Latina woman with the richness of her experiences would more often than not reach a better conclusion than a white male who hasn't lived that life.
Sonia Sotomayor

If someone betrays you once, it's their fault; if they betray you twice, it's your fault.
Eleanor Roosevelt

If you want to be a successful in this world, you have to follow your passion, not a paycheck.
Jen Welter

People underestimate me. They always have, and maybe that's for the best. It's fun to prove them wrong.
Jennifer Lopez

The only things one can admire at length are those one admires without knowing why.
Eleanor Roosevelt

Young women should pave their own path. I find it quite confining to live up to anybody else's expectations of who you should be.
Jessica Alba

Destiny is a name often given in retrospect to choices that had dramatic consequences.
J.K. Rowling

The work of today is the history of tomorrow, and we are its makers.
Juliette Gordon Low

We need women who are so strong they can be gentle, so educated they can be humble, so fierce they can be compassionate, so passionate they can be rational, and so disciplined they can be free.
Kavita Ramdas

My experiences remind me that it's those black clouds that make the blue skies even more beautiful.
Kelly Clarkson

Life is like a coin. You can spend it any way you wish, but you only spend it once.
Lillian Dickson

Think as little as possible about yourself. Think as much as possible about other people.
Eleanor Roosevelt

The universe might respect the law of attraction, but it respects a good hustle even more.
Lilly Singh

We are all just doing the best we know how with the understanding, awareness, knowledge we have at the time.
Louise Hay

Write what should not be forgotten.
Isabel Allende

Maybe you have to know the darkness before you can appreciate the light.
Madeleine L'Engle

In the long run, we shape our lives, and we shape ourselves. The process never ends until we die. And the choices we make are ultimately our own responsibility.
Eleanor Roosevelt

There are years that ask questions and years that answer.
Zora Neale Hurston

I have the same goal I've had ever since I was a girl. I want to rule the world.
Madonna

I see myself hitting all the routines, doing everything perfectly. I imagine all the moves and go through them in my mind.
Mary Lou Renton

A great soul serves everyone all the time A great soul never dies. It brings us together again and again.
Maya Angelou

My experience has been that work is almost the best way to pull oneself out of the depths.
Eleanor Roosevelt

In this life, to earn your place you have to fight for it.
Shakira

Those who truly care for you will linger, accept, and understand you.
Mayra Betances

A woman with a voice is by definition a strong woman. But the search to find that voice can be remarkably difficult.
Melinda Gates

I've found that the first thirty minutes of my day have the biggest impact on how I feel for the rest of my waking hours.
Molli Sullivan

We all create the person we become by our choices as we go through life. In a real sense, by the time we are adults, we are the sum total of the choices we have made.
Eleanor Roosevelt

Sometimes the bad things that happen in our lives put us directly on the path to the most wonderful things that will ever happen to us.
Nicole Reed

So fine was the morning except for a streak of wind here and there that the sea and sky looked all one fabric, as if sails were stuck high up in the sky, or the clouds had dropped down into the sea.
Virginia Woolf

You don't go around grieving all the time, but the grief is still there and always will be.
Nigella Lawson

Revenge only engenders violence, not clarity and true peace. I think liberation must come from within.
Sandra Cisneros

Be thankful for what you have; you'll end up having more. If you concentrate on what you don't have, you will never, ever have enough.
Oprah Winfrey

Friendship with one's self is all-important because, without it, one cannot be friends with anyone else in the world.
Eleanor Roosevelt

The thing that gives you the competitive edge is the history and relationships you have with your customers.
Professor Moira Clark

Positive things can come from painful experiences.
Maria Teresa Ramos and Sandra L. Ramos-Magnani

Wishing you strength for today and hope for tomorrow.
Renee Oneill

I don't think being beautiful takes away from your credibility.
Soledad O'Brien

My hope is that I will take the good from my experiences and extrapolate them further into areas with which I am unfamiliar. I simply do not know exactly what that difference will be in my judging. But I accept there will be some based on my gender and my Latina heritage.
Sonia Sotomayor

Many people will walk in and out of your life, but only true friends will leave footprints in your heart.
Eleanor Roosevelt

Think like a queen. A queen is not afraid to fail. Failure is another stepping stone to greatness.
Oprah Winfrey

The silence in the morning holds lots of expectations and is more hopeful than the silence at night.
Victoria Durnak

CHAPTER 4

Dreams

Today dreaming for me is a leitmotif, that alternate reality that always appears and is transformed into life, stroke, and certainty. It is not an afterlife; it is close to perennial. So many things have been formed and been made possible just by thinking of them.

Artist

We know that dreaming is for free ... but sometimes we need to give freedom to our mind, spirit, heart, and simply dream like children. Always thinking big brings us closer to our dreams. These are the most desired and expected that awaken from sleep; make us work and pursue our goals and desires.

We must never stop dreaming!

Author

Quotes About Dreams

The sacred is not in heaven or far away. It is all around us, and small human rituals can connect us to its presence. And of course, the greatest challenge (and gift) is to see the sacred in each other.
Alma Luz Villanueva

At the end of the day, we can endure much more than we think we can.
Frida Kahlo

You can be a thousand different women. It's your choice which one you want to be. It's about freedom and sovereignty. You celebrate who you are. You say, "This is my kingdom."
Salma Hayek

Never do things others can do and will do if there are things others cannot do or will not do.
Amelia Earhart

We are valedictorians and honor students. We are college graduates, bankers, police officers, entertainers, teachers, journalists, politicians, and we are the future of America.
America Ferrera

You only have what you give. It's by spending yourself that you become rich.
Isabel Allende

As you grow older, you will discover that you have two hands, one for helping yourself, the other for helping others.
Audrey Hepburn

If you aren't good at loving yourself, you will have a difficult time loving anyone, since you'll resent the time and energy you give another person that you aren't even giving to yourself.
Barbara De Angelis

From that time on, the world was hers for the reading. She would never be lonely again, never miss the lack of intimate friends. Books became her friends and there was one for every mood.
Betty Smith

We put so much of our time and energy into making sure that we meet everyone's expectations and into caring about what other people think of us, that we are often left feeling angry, resentful and fearful.
Brené Brown

Life is hard. It is not too short; it is too long. But you have to learn how to live; you have to have a sense of humor.
Carolina Herrera

A woman who writes has power, and a woman with power is feared.
Gloria E. Anzaldúa

If I have a single flower for every time I think about you, I could walk forever in my garden.
Claudia Adrienne Grandi

My heart dances with joy when I think about you.
Debasish Mridha

No matter how hard your rock bottom is, you can rise above it and come back.
Demi Lovato

Everyone has inside of him a piece of good news. The good news is that you don't know how great you can be! How much you can love! What you can accomplish! And what your potential is!
Anne Frank

Get behind other people's success. Your life was built on other people's dreams, so let's not let them down.
Dionicia Nava

I had the epiphany that laughter was light, and light was laughter, and that this was the secret of the universe.
Donna Tartt

Only a moment you stayed, but what an imprint your footprints have left on our hearts.
Dorothy Ferguson

With the new day comes new strength and new thoughts.
Eleanor Roosevelt

No life is so hard that you can't make it easier by the way you take it.
Ellen Glasgow

I realized how Latina I was, and then also, at the same time, how not Latina enough I was, because I'm born and raised in Los Angeles. I speak Spanish, but I don't speak perfect Spanish, not like a native speaker.
America Ferrera

This was the last astronaut job that was not (yet) done by a woman. Now with this milestone we can focus on the fact that what is important to succeed in life, it does not matter whether you are a man or a woman.
Ellen Ochoa

Grab a coffee. Journal your intentions. Get to work. Create miracles.
Elyse Santilli

Though we tremble before uncertain futures, may we meet illness, death and adversity with strength. May we dance in the face of our fears.
Gloria Anzaldúa

Collaboration, creativity, and respect build life-long connections that matter and make a difference, propelling us to work together across all boundaries.
Diane Luna

The Latina spirit translates to every aspect of our lives, from beauty to work to family. We're loving, we're loud, and we're beautiful in our essence.
Eva Longoria

My genetics gave me a curvy figure, and I've come to understand that in the Latina culture, that is beautiful.
Demi Lovato

I tried to drown my sorrows, but the bastards learned how to swim, and now I am overwhelmed by this decent and good feeling.
Frida Kahlo

Nowadays, hoy en día, with our world full of war and violence and lack of love, a world full of greed, a world full of domination, grasping power, venal stupidity, real evil, don't get me started, it's good to know that a conversation about tacos will always engender a sense of comfort and happiness. If we could only sit down at a big, round world table and eat tacos in a spirit of love, we might begin to work on world peace.
Denise Chavez

If we don't change, we don't grow. If we don't grow, we aren't really living.
Gail Sheehy

Create the highest and greatest vision possible for your life, because you become what you believe in.
Oprah Winfrey

The most difficult thing in the world is to start a career known only for your looks, and then to try to become a serious actress. No one will take you seriously once you are known as the pretty woman.
Penélope Cruz

Never give up. Always find a reason to keep trying.
Kelly Mizell

My mom was a source of strength. She showed me by example that women, regardless of how difficult life may get, can do it all.
Gloria Estefan

We are needed. We have to be engaged and get ourselves elected to school boards and city councils. Sí se puede!"
Dolores Huerta

There's no better way to tell others that they can win than by living your dreams.
Gina Rodriguez

I would like to show the world today as an ant sees it and tomorrow as the moon sees it.
Hannah Hoch

It is important to stand up for your rights, and regardless of who you are and where you come from, to hold your head up high with dignity and respect.
Hilda Solis

I can promise you that women working together, linked, informed, and educated, can bring peace to this forsaken planet.
Isabel Allende

I leave you my portrait so that you will have my presence all the days and nights that I am away from you.
Frida Kahlo

There is a part of Wonder Woman inside me and inside every woman, kind of that secret self that women share. We are all caretakers, giving birth, caring for our children and companions and loved ones.
Lynda Carter

You pierce my soul. I am half agony. Half hope. Tell me not that I am too late, that such precious feelings are gone forever.
Jane Austen

I like a lot of love and attention. I don't need someone to buy me material things. I can buy them for myself. It's nice to get presents, but it's not a sign of love.
Jennifer Lopez

It seems to me that those songs that have been any good, I have nothing much to do with the writing of them. The words have just crawled down my sleeve and come out on the page.
Joan Baez

In response to those who say to stop dreaming and face reality, I say keep dreaming and make a reality.
Kristian Kan

The simple truth is that the truth does not exist, it all depends on a person's point of view.
Laura Esquivel

Don't ask if your dream is crazy, ask if it's crazy enough.
Lena Waithe

The thing you have to be prepared for is that other people don't always dream your dream.
Linda Ronstadt

Everyone has highs and lows that they have to learn from, but every morning I start off with a good head on my shoulders, saying to myself, 'It's going to be a good day!
Lindsay Lohan

Keep smiling, because life is a beautiful thing and there's so much to smile about.
Marilyn Monroe

You have to believe in yourself. You have to take care of yourself, work for yourself, believe in yourself, and also e patient with yourself. Learn when not to push too hard, and give yourself a break.
Selma Hayek

Don't wait until you die to be reborn. Your past does not define who you are, it's only muscle that you are building for your future.
Mayra Rubio

Heroism doesn't always happen in a burst of glory. Sometimes small triumphs and large hearts change the course of history.
Mary Roach

When you're quiet, everything settles on the floor of your mind like sediment in undisturbed still water.
Megan Monahan

Always be you — and learn to let go in order to grow. You owe it to yourself.
Vivian Martinez-Stachura

What does the brain matter compared with the heart?
Virginia Woolf

When I'm hungry, I eat what I love. When I'm bored, I do something I love. When I'm lonely, I connect with someone I love. When I feel sad, I remember that I am loved.
Michelle May

The season of mourning, like spring, summer, fall and winter, will also pass.
Molly Fumia

Make sure to do something that provides you with motivation to get up in the morning and go to work. Whether it's passion for a mission, excitement about creating, or intellectual stimulation, follow a path where you consistently feel engaged.
Nadia Abouzaid

Strive to be a person of value, and success will undeniably follow.
Nenci Rodriguez

You are valued, you are a goddess and don't forget that.
Jennifer Lopez

Follow your dreams despite what other people think, and work toward them every day.
Nydia Monarrez

I've come to believe that each of us has a personal calling that's as unique as a fingerprint —and that the best way to succeed is to discover what you love and then find a way to offer it to others in the form of service, working hard, and also allowing the energy of the universe to lead you.
Oprah Winfrey

What I wanted to express very clearly and intensely was that the reason these people had to invent or imagine heroes and gods is pure fear. Fear of life and fear of death.
Frida Kahlo

Positive thoughts bring positive outcomes.
Raisa Jimenez

Self-care doesn't necessarily mean jogging!
Sandra Oh

Your life was a blessing, your memory a treasure. You are loved beyond words and missed beyond measure.
Renee Wood

Bigger than life is not difficult for me. I am bigger than life.
Rita Moreno

The most liberating thing about beauty is realizing that you are the beholder.
Salma Hayek

I am a woman, and I am a Latina. Those are the things that make my writing distinctive. Those are the things that give my writing power.
Sandra Cisneros

Our life and our success will be measured by the quality of the life we lead and the lives we touch.
Sandra X Pradas Martin

The impossible is always possible.
Selena Quintanilla

I believe that every single one of us, celebrity or not, has a responsibility to get involved in trying to make a difference in the world.
Shakira

When you are joyful, when you say yes to life and have fun and project positivity all around you, you become a sun in the center of every constellation, and people want to be near you.
Shannon L. Adler

One can only discover what has already come into existence.
Shirley Hazzard

Believing in your talents, your abilities and your self-worth can empower you to walk down an even brighter path.
Soledad O'Brien

Your individuality is important, but so is belonging. Recognize the parts of your culture that have shaped your past, and the parts you want to carry with you into the future.
Sol Peralta

The one good thing about not seeing you is that I can write you letters.
Svetlana Alliluyeva

Stepping out of the busyness, stopping our endless pursuit of getting somewhere else, is perhaps the most beautiful offering we can make to our spirit.
Tara Brach

Spend time thinking about what matters to you and what you find to be meaningful. Invest in those things. It's wonderful when you can live your life in accordance with your own values rather than what other people tell you you should want. Leave everything else behind because it really doesn't matter if it doesn't bring you joy.
Tasha Cochran

Have a dream, chase it down, jump over every single hurdle, and run through fire and ice to get there.
Whitney Wolfe Herd

CHAPTER 5

Courage

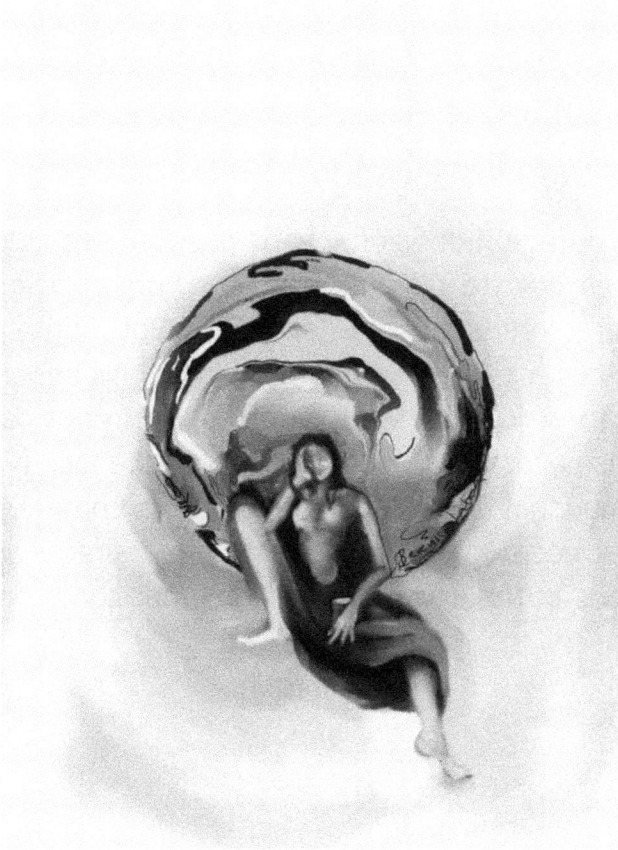

The one that is needed to face the *emptiness* that luminous, smooth, and perfect canvas, either from the front, from the side or simply spilling; that first stroke is with courage.

Artist

With courage, decision, and passion we can make decisions despite difficulties. Every human being carries courage internally by nature. But unfortunately, sometimes, we ourselves do not realize this important and necessary value that we have, to apply in our day-to-day life. It is necessary to have courage in the face of physical and emotional pain. It sometimes takes courage to make the best decisions for ourselves. With courage we can be victorious in the complex situations that come our way in life.

Author

Quotes on Courage

I have sometimes been wildly, despairingly, acutely miserable, racked with sorrow, but through it all I still know quite certainly that just to be alive is a grand thing.
Agatha Christie

I want to walk through life instead of being dragged through it.
Alanis Morissette

Nothing is worth more than laughter. It is strength to laugh and to abandon oneself, to be light. Tragedy is the most ridiculous thing.
Frida Kahlo

You gain strength, courage, and confidence by every experience in which you really stop to look fear in the face.
Eleanor Roosevelt

Life shrinks or expands in proportion to one's courage.
Anais Nin

The thing that is really hard, and really amazing, is giving up on being perfect and beginning the work of becoming yourself.
Anna Quindlen

Almost everything will work again if you unplug it for a few minutes ... including you.
Anne Lamott

All your power resides in the now. Mindfulness is the best tool to tap you into that power.
Anita M. Scott

We've all had stress creep up on us without even noticing it until we lost it on someone who didn't deserve it, and then we realize that we probably should have checked in with ourselves a little earlier.
Ariel Garten

Self-care isn't selfish. It's self-esteem.
Ashley Judd

The courage to be vulnerable is not about winning or losing, it's about the courage to show up when you can't predict or control the outcome.
Brené Brown

All my life, because I'm blonde and blue-eyed, people who aren't Hispanic can't believe I am. And people who are Hispanic always think I'm not, because I don't look like them. Being Latin is part of who I am and I bring that part to every role.
Cameron Diaz

Whatever it is that you think you want to do, and whatever it is that you think stands between you and that, stop making excuses. You can do anything.
Katia Beauchamp

Whatever happens to you belongs to you. Make it yours. Feed it to yourself even if it feels impossible to swallow. Let it nurture you because it will.
Cheryl Strayed

A really strong woman accepts the war she went through and is ennobled by her scars.
Carly Simon

Since you get more joy out of giving joy to others, you should put a good deal of thought into the happiness you are able to give.
Eleanor Roosevelt

For my part, I am almost contented just now, and very thankful. Gratitude is a divine emotion: it fills the heart, but not to bursting; it warms it, but not to fever.
Charlotte Brontë

I think women are sensual, beautiful beings, and I feel empowered when I express myself sexually.
Christina Aguilera

Our fear was not as strong as our courage.
Malala Yousafzai

If I could go back and give myself advice, I would say, "You deserve to be here because you are a good actor. You know it. Now, let everybody else know."
Daniella De Jesús

Courage is exhilarating.
Eleanor Roosevelt

Forever is composed of nows.
Emily Dickinson

Never be ashamed of what you feel. You have the right to feel any emotion that you want, and to do what makes you happy.
Demi Lovato

I'd like to see a world free of strife, stress, pain, hunger, war–a cool place where everyone could live.
Dionne Warwick

How very softly you tiptoed into our world, almost silently, only a moment you stayed. But what an imprint your footsteps have left upon our hearts.
Dorothy Ferguson

Stay strong as you live your life story and remember your blessings, no matter what circumstances you face.
Dr. Damary M. Bonilla-Rodriguez

Don't be afraid to get no's, make mistakes and fail multiple times. That's gonna give you a thicker skin to follow your passion and your own road!
Naya Rappaport

Life is challenging but I'm always up for a challenge.
Venus Williams

I always believed that women have rights and that there are some women that are intelligent enough to claim those rights. There are some others that are stupid enough not to.
Shakira

It is a brave thing to have courage to be an individual; it is also, perhaps, a lonely thing. But it is better than not being an individual, which is to be nobody at all.
Eleanor Roosevelt

It is terrifying to see the rich having parties day and night while thousands and thousands of people are dying of hunger...
Frida Kahlo

Vulnerability is the birthplace of love, belonging, joy, courage, empathy, and creativity. It is the source of hope, empathy, accountability, and authenticity. If we want greater clarity in our purpose or deeper and more meaningful spiritual lives, vulnerability is the path.
Brené Brown

There is no chance, no destiny, no fate, that can hinder or control the firm resolve of a determined soul.
Ella Wheeler Wilcox

People generally see what they look for, and hear what they listen for.
Harper Lee

These morning practices are what fuel me; keeping my routine is not about willpower.
Jenny Blake

When you're feeling frazzled, put all of your attention on the breath. It's a portal into the present moment, the best remedy for stress.
Ellen Barrett

I think that little by little I'll be able to solve my problems and survive.
Frida Kahlo

I think Hispanic women are beautiful with their curves. I'm not sure who feels that way in Hollywood. I was never told to lose 50 pounds. If they think that they just don't bother with you. You just don't get the role and you never know why. That's still better than physically harming yourself and becoming unhealthy just to star in a movie.
America Ferrera

Manners are a sensitive awareness of the feelings of others. If you have the awareness, you have good manners, no matter what fork you use.
Emily Post

I tried to drown my sorrows, but the bastards learned how to swim, and now I am overwhelmed by this decent and good feeling.
Frida Kahlo

When you tell people their situation is only 'perception' and they can change it, you shame them, belittle them and, in the case of domestic violence, you put them in extreme physical danger. Rather than dismissing someone's experience as perception, we might want to ask, 'How can I help?' or 'Is there some way I can support you?'
Brené Brown

When your mother asks, 'Do you want a piece of advice?' it is a mere formality. It doesn't matter if you answer yes or no. You're going to get it anyway.
Erma Bombeck

No need to hurry. No need to sparkle. No need to be anybody but oneself.
Virginia Woolf

I leave you my portrait so that you will have my presence all the days and nights that I am away from you.
Frida Kahlo

If you are a woman and you're assertive and you want to get the job done, you're a bitch. If you're a guy, you're just assertive.
Christina Aguilera

Part of courage is simple consistency.
Peggy Noonan

Only one mountain can know the core of another mountain.
Frida Kahlo

One of the most courageous things you can do is identify yourself, know who you are, what you believe in and where you want to go.
Sheila Murray Bethel

The most important part of the body is the brain. Of my face, I like the eyebrows and eyes.
Frida Kahlo

A pedestal is as much a prison as any small space.
Gloria Steinem

It is not fair to ask of others what you are not willing to do yourself.
Eleanor Roosevelt

People might think you can turn creativity on and off, but it's not like that. It just kind of comes out. A mash up of all these things you collect in your mind. You never know when it's gonna happen, but when it does...it's like magic. It's just that simple and it's just that hard.
Gwen Stefani

I wanted you to see what real courage is, instead of getting the idea that courage is a man with a gun in his hand. It's when you know you're licked before you begin but you begin anyway and you see it through no matter what. You rarely win, but sometimes you do.
Harper Lee

Never bend your head. Always hold it high. Look the world straight in the face.
Helen Keller

To lose someone you love is to alter your life forever. You don't get over it because 'it' is the person you loved. The pain stops, there are new people, but the gap never closes. How could it? [...] This hole in my heart is in the shape of you and no one else can fit it.
Jeanette Winterson

I am a woman like any other and ugly things happen to me like any other women.
Jenni Rivera

I was a child who went about in a world of colors... My friends, my companions, became women slowly; I became old in instants.
Frida Kahlo

When you stand up in front of an audience, you should say a lot about a little — don't say a little about a lot.
Kimberley Clark

Ethics, decency, and morality are the real soldiers.
Kiran Bedi

Take chances, make mistakes — that is how we grow. Pain nourishes your courage. You have to fail in order to practice being brave.
Mary Tyler Moore

There are no have-to's, just choices.
Eleanor Roosevelt

Honestly, self-care is not fluffy. It's something we should take seriously.
Kris Carr

I am not afraid of storms, for I am learning how to sail my ship.
Louisa May Alcott

I'm pretty but I'm not beautiful. I sin but I'm not the devil. I'm good, but I'm not an angel.
Marilyn Monroe

Courage does not always roar. Sometimes courage is the quiet voice at the end of the day saying, "I'll try again tomorrow."
Mary Ann Radmacher

If you don't like something, change it. If you can't change it, change your attitude.
Maya Angelou

They thought I was a Surrealist, but I wasn't. I never painted dreams. I painted my own reality.
Frida Kahlo

A thousand moments that I had just taken for granted, mostly because I had assumed that there would be a thousand more.
Morgan Matson

I was going through puberty and was much curvier than other girls, which made me insecure. Then I saw J. Lo on the cover of 'Latina' magazine, and she embraced those curves and was proud of who she was.
Nikki Bella

Courage isn't something you are born with. It comes to you with experience.
Patricia Neal

I'm a big fan of the saying, "Nothing beats a failure but a try."
Regina King

I hope the exit is joyful. And I hope never to return.
Frida Kahlo

If only the sun-drenched celebrities are being noticed and worshiped, then our children are going to have a tough time seeing the value in the shadows, where the thinkers, probers, and scientists are keeping society together.
Rita Dove

It's not the lucky ones who succeed. It's the ones who decide to go after what they really want.
Shaina Leis

Whether born from experience or inherent physiological or cultural differences, our gender and national origins may and will make a difference in our judging.
Sonia Sotomayor

Encourage yourself, believe in yourself, and love yourself. Never doubt who you are.
Stephanie LaHart

What I wanted to express very clearly and intensely was that the reason these people had to invent or imagine heroes and gods is pure fear. Fear of life and fear of death.
Frida Kahlo

Success, they taught me, is built on the foundation of courage, hard work, and individual responsibility. Despite what some would have us believe, success is not built on resentment and fears.
Susana Martinez

It has been so important for me to embrace what I personally bring to the table. Let your stories inform your voice.
Vivian Nuñez

My painting carries with it the message of pain.
Frida Kahlo

People think of Latina women as being fiery and fierce, which is usually true. But I think the quality that so many Latinas possess is strength. I'm very proud to have Latin blood.
Zoe Saldana

CHAPTER 6

Freedom

Decide whether to paint or not. There is no need for my painting. Nobody dies and nobody forces me. However, there are fillers in me that want to talk to me about something. It starts from scratch or it overlaps. It is created out of nothing or we resort to that spiral in which we rewind. But we also evolve, dream and thus I am free to repeat myself or to renew myself.

Artist

Freedom does not have a price! But in turn, it is the right that all human beings have, to choose our own way of acting within a society. We are free to have different values, criteria, wishes and objectives. It is the prime outlet of human beings to use writing to represent the idea of **"freedom."**

Author

Freedom Quotes

Great Being Latina to me is living your life like it's a big old fiesta!
Adrienne Bailon

I am who I am today because of the choices I made yesterday.
Eleanor Roosevelt

We Latin women are liberated from the neck up, not the neck down.
Cristina Saralegui

Understand this, I mean to arrive at the truth. The truth, however ugly in itself, is always curious and beautiful to seekers after it.
Agatha Christie

I am my own woman.
Eva Peron

What you perceive as "liberal" is my independence to choose what I do, with whom and when. Moreover, it also means that I may choose not to do it, with anyone, ever.
Ana Castillo

We turn not older with years but newer every day.
Emily Dickinson

Almost everything will work again if you unplug it for a few minutes, including you.
Anne Lamott

Knowing how to be solitary is central to the art of loving. When we can be alone, we can be with others without using them as a means of escape.
Bell Hooks

Life imposes things on you that you can't control, but you still have the choice of how you're going to live through this.
Celine Dion

You are joy, looking for a way to express.
Esther Hicks

Self-care means giving yourself permission to pause.
Cecilia Tran

I am no bird; and no net ensnares me: I am a free human being with an independent will, which I now exert to leave you.
Charlotte Brontë

My painting carries with it the message of pain.
Frida Kahlo

Practicing a mindful moment in the middle of the day, helps to bring you back to center, reset, and move into the rest of your day with greater clarity and focus.
Christine Agro

I don't care what you think about me. I don't think about you at all.
Coco Chanel

Never allow a person to tell you no who doesn't have the power to say yes.
Eleanor Roosevelt

It might sound dramatic and a little grandiose, but as a Latina, I would like to be someone that gives a voice to my culture.
Cristela Alonzo

Feel the feeling but don't become the emotion. Witness it. Allow it. Release it.
Crystal Andrus

For the next month do not criticize yourself with your words or your thoughts. Imagine a month of nothing but self-praise for who you are and what you do.
Diane Osagie

You may be disappointed if you fail, but you are doomed if you don't try.
Beverly Sills

Take a lover who looks at you like maybe you are a bourbon biscuit.
Frida Kahlo

It's all about falling in love with yourself and sharing that love with someone who appreciates you, rather than looking for love to compensate for a self-love deficit.
Eartha Kitt

Do not stop thinking of life as an adventure. You have no security unless you can live bravely, excitingly, imaginatively; unless you can choose a challenge instead of competence.
Eleanor Roosevelt

It allows others to be responsible for themselves and for us to take our hands-off situations that do not belong to us. This frees us from unnecessary stress.
Melody Beattie

For many years, my morning routine was a result of how other people expected me to show up. I was overwhelmed and off-center because I was ignoring the messages my body was sending me.
Amber Rae

Life is an endurance sport, but endurance without compassion is torture. Living mindfully, we bring our whole heart to the event of being alive so that we can be present from beginning to end.
Lauren Eckstrom

There is enormous power in nailing your morning routine, but there's even more power in adapting to it when it doesn't happen as we'd like.
Terri Schneider

Unable are the loved to die, for love is immortality.
Emily Dickinson

Love yourself, have dignity, know your worth and don't settle.
Wendy Rodriguez

Among poor people, there's not any question about women being strong — even stronger than men — they work in the fields right along with the men. When your survival is at stake, you don't have these questions about yourself like middle-class women do.
Dolores Huerta

Whether the day is for writing, designing, or painting, the consistent practice of a morning routine is the doorway into it all.
Elle Luna

The most important thing in your life is to live your life with integrity and to not give into peer pressure to try to be something that you're not.
Ellen DeGeneres

Nothing has ever been achieved by the person who says, 'It can't be done.'
Eleanor Roosevelt

The greatest gift you can ever give another person is your own happiness.
Esther Hicks

The Latina spirit translates to every aspect of our lives, from beauty to work to family. We're loving, we're loud, and we're beautiful in our essence.
Eva Longoria

The longer I live, the more uninformed I feel. Only the young have an explanation for everything.
Isabel Allende

In order to succeed, you can't be afraid to fail. Just do it and don't let anybody tell you you can't.
Faith Hill

Latin women are very comfortable with their bodies and their sexuality. We aren't afraid to show that off a little bit more.
Sofia Vergara

Pain, pleasure and death are no more than a process for existence. The revolutionary struggle in this process is a doorway open to intelligence.
Frida Kahlo

I want to steer away from the stereotypes that Latina women are categorized in. I feel like there are so many more opportunities for us. I like going out for those roles that says 'open ethnicity.
Emily Rios

Freedom makes a huge requirement of every human being. With freedom comes responsibility. For the person who is unwilling to grow up, the person who does not want to carry his own weight, this is a frightening prospect.
Eleanor Roosevelt

It is important to have strong images of women out there, women who aren't afraid of expressing themselves, women who aren't' afraid of taking chances, women who aren't afraid of their own power.
Gina Torres

The beautiful spring came; and when Nature resumes her loveliness, the human soul is apt to revive also.
Harriett Ann Jacobs

What we have once enjoyed we can never lose. All that we love deeply becomes a part of us.
Helen Keller

Always make decisions that prioritize your inner peace.
Izey Victoria Odiase

Live in the moment, day by day, and don't stress about the future. People are so caught up in looking into the future that they kind of lose what's in front of them.
Jenna Ushkowitz

Life was meant to be lived, and curiosity must be kept alive. One must never, for whatever reason, turn his back on life.
Eleanor Roosevelt

The point is not to pay back kindness, but to pass it on.
Julia Alvarez

What's truly important...is that right here, right now, I am free.
Kat Von D

In any free society, the conflict between social conformity and individual liberty is permanent, unresolvable, and necessary.
Kathleen Norris

Whoever controls information, whoever controls meaning, acquires power.
Laura Esquivel

We are all just doing the best we know how with the understanding, awareness, knowledge we have at the time.
Louise Hay

Accept the children the way we accept trees; with gratitude because they are a blessing. But do not have expectations or desires. You don't expect trees to change; you love them as they are.
Isabel Allende

The thing that makes you exceptional, if you are at all, is inevitably that which must also make you lonely.
Lorraine Hansberry

What is fundamentally beautiful is compassion, for yourself and those around you.
Lupita Nyong'o

Life, with its rules, its obligations, and its freedoms, is like a sonnet: You're given the form, but you have to write the sonnet yourself.
Madeleine L'Engle

Strong women don't play the victim. Don't make themselves look pitiful and don't point fingers. They stand and they deal.
Mandy Hale

We were the people who were not in the papers. We lived in the blank white spaces at the edges of print. It gave us more freedom. We lived in the gaps between the stories.
Margaret Atwood

Service is the rent we pay for being. It is the very purpose of life, and not something you do in your spare time.
Marian Wright Edelman

One thing life has taught me: if you are interested, you never have to look for new interests. They come to you. When you are genuinely interested in one thing, it will always lead to something else.
Eleanor Roosevelt

Don't limit yourself. Many people limit themselves to what they think they can do. You can go as far as your mind lets you. What you believe, remember, you can achieve.
Mary Kay Ash

Women are leaders everywhere you look— from the CEO who runs a Fortune 500 company to the housewife who raises her children and heads her household. Our country was built by strong women, and we will continue to break down walls and defy stereotypes.
Nancy Pelosi

There's a lot of stress out there, and to handle it, you just need to believe in yourself; always go back to the person that you know you are, and don't let anybody tell you any different, because everyone's special and everyone's awesome.
McKayla Maroney

I have to represent. I feel proud to have a culture that's different... and proud to be a Latina. We're not all categorized as one type of person... there's people from everywhere doing different things who have different types of cultures. Being Latina for me is also being a strong woman.
Natalie Martinez

Above all, be the heroine of your life, not the victim.
Nora Ephron

I never waste time looking back.
Eleanor Roosevelt

One must take what comes, with laughter.
Olivia de Havilland

Give yourself a moment to come to rest, pause, and collect yourself.
Rhonda Magee

Expect the unexpected, but celebrate anyway.
Taylor Swift

We have to laugh, because laughter, we already know, is the first evidence of freedom.
Rosario Castellanos

We can climb mountains with self-love.
Samira Wiley

Since everybody is an individual, nobody can be you. You are unique. No one can tell you how to use your time. It is yours. Your life is your own. You mold it. You make it.
Eleanor Roosevelt

When you are joyful, when you say yes to life and have fun and project positivity all around you, you become a sun in the center of every constellation, and people want to be near you.
Shannon L. Adler

A free woman is just the opposite of an easy woman.
Simone de Beauvoir

Never take no personally. Sometimes people tell you no for a reason that has nothing to do with you. You must keep going.
Sofía Vergara

Introverts prefer to devote their social energies to close friends, colleagues, and family.
Susan Cain

Mindfulness is the aware, balanced acceptance of the present experience. It isn't more complicated than that. It is opening to or receiving the present moment, pleasant or unpleasant, just as it is, without either clinging to it or rejecting it.
Sylvia Boorstein

We have to face the fact that either all of us are going to die together or we are going to learn to live together, and if we are to live together, we have to talk.
Eleanor Roosevelt

Those we love and lose are always connected by heartstrings into infinity.
Terri Guillemets

Happiness is a choice. You can choose to be happy. There's going to be stress in life, but it's your choice whether you let it affect you or not.
Valerie Bertinelli

Mornings are so precious because lñ when I'm most productive. For me, thirty minutes at 5:30am is equivalent to at least an hour at 3:00pm.
Whitney Johnson

CHAPTER 7

Beliefs

The hope in the dream of a work is the first part of creating. The next part is having the courage to go for it. This grows with the freedom to decide another path or by staying persistent with the idea. Passion is added and lived internally and then shown to the audience, causing believing and creating to become one.

Artist

Belief is when we accept something that is true, according to our own perspective. It is the assumption or thought that we have about things, people, situations, and when we believe in something or someone. It also refers to when we accept or affirm something without having tangible proof that it is true or perhaps not. Believing always comforts the soul.

Author

Quotes About Beliefs

Time moves slowly, but passes quickly.
Alice Walker

The most effective way to do is to do it.
Amelia Earhart

You can't use up creativity. The more you use, the more you have.
Maya Angelou

We think, mistakenly, that success is the result of the amount of time we put in at work, instead of the quality of time we put in.
Arianna Huffington

Hate and force cannot be in just a part of the world without having an effect on the rest of it.
Eleanor Roosevelt

When I dare to be powerful, to use my strength in the service of my vision, then it becomes less and less important whether I am afraid.
Audre Lorde

The most important thing is to enjoy your life – to be happy – it's all that matters.
Audrey Hepburn

When people tell you not to believe in your dreams, and they say "Why?", say "Why not?
Billie Jean King

Perfectionism is self-destructive simply because there's no such thing as perfect. Perfection is an unattainable goal.
Brené Brown

Woman is the dominant sex. Men have to do all sorts of stuff to prove they are worthy of a woman's attention.
Camille Pagla

The impossible does not exist for a woman, it only takes time to achieve it.
Carolina Herrera

Remember-works of love are works of peace.
Mother Teresa

Don't ever make decisions based on fear. Make decisions based on hope and possibility. Make decisions based on what should happen, not what shouldn't.
Michelle Obama

Be kind to your wandering mind.
Diana Winston

We are all the pieces of what we remember. We hold in ourselves the hopes and fears of those who love us. As long as there is love and memory, there is no true loss
Cassandra Clare

Stress is an ignorant state. It believes that everything is an emergency. Nothing is that important.
Natalie Goldberg

Create the highest and greatest vision possible for your life, because you become what you believe in.
Oprah Winfrey

So often people are working hard at the wrong thing. Working on the right thing is probably more important than working hard.
Caterina Fake

Let me wake up next to you, have coffee in the morning and wander through the city with your hand in mine, and I'll be happy for the rest of my little life.
Charlotte Eriksson

For safety is not a gadget but a state of mind.
Eleanor Everet

If you want to live an authentic, meaningful life, you need to master the art of disappointing and upsetting others, hurting feelings, and living with the reality that some people just won't like you. It may not be easy, but it's essential if you want your life to reflect your deepest desires, values, and needs.
Cheryl Richardson

Sometimes you can't see yourself clearly until you see yourself through the eyes of others.
Ellen DeGeneres

There's always a sunrise and always a sunset and it's up to you to choose to be there for it,' said my mother. 'Put yourself in the way of beauty.
Cheryl Strayed

When I am lonely, I think of you and all that you brought to my life. Your memory rests gently on my soul.
Cindy Adkins

For the next month do not criticize yourself with your words or your thoughts. Imagine a month of nothing but self-praise – praise for who you are and what you do.
Diana Osagie

I had the epiphany that laughter was light, and light was laughter, and that this was the secret of the universe.
Donna Tartt

In essence, doubt gives you time for your brain to catch up with your soul. It is an important, significant part of the faith process.
Dr. Adele Ryan McDowell

The Ability to find the funny pumps oxygen into adverse situations. Whit humor, we can live our lives a little more honestly, and less fearfully, even though we can't make bad things go away.
Elaine Smookler

In all our contacts it is probably the sense of being really needed and wanted which gives us the greatest satisfaction and creates the most lasting bond.
Eleanor Roosevelt

Be happy in the moment. That is enough.
Mother Teresa

You take your problems to a god, but what you really need is for the god to take you to the inside of you.
Tina Turner

Believing in yourself and fighting for your dreams is what enables you to live each day and face every obstacle.
Yaneli Sosa

You can never really live anyone else's life, not even your child's. The influence you exert is through your own life, and what you've become yourself.
Eleanor Roosevelt

On my own I will just create, and if it works, it works, and if it doesn't, I'll create something else. I don't have any limitations on what I think I could do or be.
Oprah Winfrey

Your morning sets up the success of your day. So many people wake up and immediately check text messages, emails, and social media. I use my first hour awake for my morning routine of breakfast and meditation to prepare myself.
Caroline Ghosn

Today is the oldest you've ever been, and the youngest you'll ever be again.
Eleanor Roosevelt

Once you figure out who you are and what you love about yourself, I think it all kinda falls into place.
Jennifer Aniston

I believe anyone can conquer fear by doing the things he fears to do, provided he keeps doing them until he gets a record of successful experience behind him.
Eleanor Roosevelt

For me, every hour is grace. And I feel gratitude in my heart each time I can meet someone and look at his or her smile.
Elie Wiesel

Whatever is being experienced, just allow it and let it be.
Elisha Goldstein

I think I deserve something beautiful.
Elizabeth Gilbert

Girls should never be afraid to be smart.
Emma Watson

You deserve the best, the very best, because you are one of the few people in this lousy world who are honest to themselves, and that is the only thing that really counts.
Frida Kahlo

Surround yourself with people who believe in you more than you do in yourself.
Gaby Natale

I know now that we never get over great losses; we absorb them, and they carve us into different, often kinder, creatures.
Gail Caldwell

Roots are not in landscape or a country, or a people. They are inside you.
Isabel Allende

Grief and love are conjoined—you don't get one without the other.
Jandy Nelson

You pierce my soul. I am half agony. Half hope. Tell me not that I am too late, that such precious feelings are gone forever.
Jane Austen

In my experience, there is only one motivation, and that is desire. No reasons or principle contain it or stand against it.
Jane Smiley

Before we can make friends with anyone else, we must first make friends with ourselves.
Eleanor Roosevelt

When you recover or discover something that nourishes your soul and brings joy, care enough about yourself to make room for it in your life.
Jean Shinoda Bolen

Live in the moment, day by day, and don't stress about the future. People are so caught up in looking into the future that they kind of lose what's in front of them.
Jenna Ushkowitz

There are no regrets in life. Just lessons.
Jennifer Aniston

As for my girls, I'll raise them to think they breathe fire.
Jessica Kirkland

Life is a fairytale starring you. You have the power to write your own story and be the hero of it, too.
Joelle Speranza

What could we accomplish if we knew we could not fail?
Eleanor Roosevelt

A positive attitude gives you power over your circumstances instead of your circumstances having power over you.
Joyce Meyer

Anxiety happens when you think you have to figure out everything all at once. Breathe. You're strong. You got this. Take it day by day.
Karen Salmansohn

Loving yourself isn't vanity. It's sanity.
Katrina Mayer

Perhaps the only thing in my favor is that I am very tenacious.
I don't take "no" very well.
Kathryn Bigelow

I work really hard at trying to see the big picture and not getting
stuck in ego. I believe we're all put on this planet for a purpose,
and we all have a different purpose. When you connect with that
love and that compassion, that's when everything unfolds.
Ellen DeGeneres

It isn't enough to talk about peace. One must believe in it. And
it isn't enough to believe in it. One must work at it.
Eleanor Roosevelt

Surrender to things you cannot change from your past, release
your worries of tomorrow, and learn to value the present and
inner peace will follow.
Kenia Nunez

If you don't think your anxiety, depression, sadness and stress
impact your physical health, think again. All of these emotions
trigger chemical reactions in your body, which can lead to
inflammation and a weakened immune system. Learn how to
cope, sweet friend.
Kris Carr

When we allow ourselves to embrace the moment, we allow
ourselves to live.
Lisa Bien

Sometimes you just need to be selfish to be self-sufficient.
Lois P. Frankel

Keep good company, read good books, love good things, and cultivate soul and body as faithfully as you can.
Louisa May Alcott

You have to accept whatever comes, and the only important thing is that you meet it with the best you have to give.
Eleanor Roosevelt

You can't truly heal from a loss until you allow yourself to really feel the loss.
Mandy Hale

Tomorrow I'll think of some way to get him back. After all, tomorrow is another day.
Margaret Mitchell

You need to be able to manage stress because hard times will come, and a positive outlook is what gets you through.
Marie Osmond

It is a serious thing – just to be alive – on this fresh morning – in this broken world.
Mary Oliver

As you grow older, you will discover that you have two hands, one for helping yourself, the other for helping others.
Maya Angelou

This a wonderful day. I've never seen this one before.
Maya Angelou

When you have decided what you believe, what you feel must be done, have the courage to stand alone and be counted.
Eleanor Roosevelt

Gratitude makes sense of our past, brings peace for today, and creates a vision for tomorrow.
Melody Beattie

Life is not easy for any of us. But what of that? We must have perseverance and, above all, confidence in ourselves. We must believe that we are gifted for something, and that this thing, at whatever cost, must be attained.
Marie Curie

Find people who will make you better.
Michelle Obama

There is no sunrise so beautiful that it is worth waking me up to see it.
Mindy Kaling

The moment when you first wake up in the morning is the most wonderful of the 24 hours. No matter how weary or dreary you may feel, you possess the certainty that, during the day that lies before you, absolutely anything may happen. And the fact that it practically always doesn't, matters not a jot. The possibility is always there.
Monica Baldwin

The fruit of silence is prayer,
The fruit of prayer is faith,
The fruit of faith is love,
The fruit of love is service,
The fruit of service is peace.
Mother Teresa

Some losses don't hurt just for a while, they hurt for a lifetime.
Narin Grewal

There will never be a day when I won't think of you and wish you were here by my side.
Narin Grewal

Remember always that you not only have the right to be an individual, you have an obligation to be one.
Eleanor Roosevelt

Breathe. Let go. And remind yourself that this very moment is the only one you know you have for sure.
Oprah Winfrey

You are the sky. Everything else is just the weather.
Pema Chodron

I have a lot to be thankful for. I am healthy, happy and I am loved.
Reba McEntire

The sun is a daily reminder that we too can rise again from the darkness, that we too can shine our own light.
S. Ajna

People who love themselves come across as very loving, generous and kind; they express their self-confidence through humility, forgiveness and inclusiveness.
Sanaya Roman

Life is like a parachute jump; you've got to get it right the first time.
Eleanor Roosevelt

To accept ourselves as we are means to value our imperfections as much as our perfections.
Sandra Bierig

You have to dance a little bit before you step out into the world each day because it changes the way you walk.
Sandra Bullock

It is in the early morning hour that the unseen is seen, and that the far-off beauty and glory, vanquishing all their vagueness, move down upon us till they stand clear as crystal close over against the soul.
Sarah Smiley

Out of the greatest respect and compassion for yourself, practice letting go and offering loving-kindness.
Sharon Salzberg

I guess at the end of the day, all women like to be appreciated and treated with respect and kindness.
Sofia Vergara

Surrender to what is. Let go of what was. Have faith in what will be.
Sonia Ricotti

And may the odds be ever in your favor.
Suzanne Collins

There are no mistakes, only opportunities.
Tina Fey

The future belongs to those who believe in the beauty of their dreams.
Eleanor Roosevelt

Self-love has very little to do with how you feel about your outer self. It's about accepting all of yourself.
Tyra Banks

CHAPTER 8

Challenges

Painting was born as a challenge. Today the simple existence is a challenge. We go through so many "us" and I wonder where I am planted; this is such a back-to-back exercise. Paint realism or just express? Trace what happened yesterday or look for what I don't know? That which makes me uncomfortable and makes me move, sometimes leaping and at times in so many trembling barely perceptible movements that seek to touch unknown threads.

Artist

Life is a total and complete challenge, but without that daily adrenaline it wouldn't have the same meaning. When we challenge ourselves and others before a competition or perhaps rivalry, a unique and even fun game begins to know who refers to compete, challenge, or provoke someone. A challenge is also a competition where a rivalry is revealed.

Author

Quotes on Challenges

A day without you is like a day without sunshine. A life without you is like a life without music. You are the sunshine on my face and the music in my heart.
Alfiya Shaliheen

Vulnerability is about sharing our feelings and our experiences with people who have earned the right to hear them.
Brené Brown

Every small positive change we make in ourselves repays us in confidence in the future.
Alice Walker

Understanding is a two-way street.
Eleanor Roosevelt

Never do things others can do and will do if there are things others cannot do or will not do.
Amelia Earhart

I bring a lot of passion to my life and my politics. I don't mind saying there is a very strong Latin component to it.
Cristina Fernandez de Kirchner

I'm a Latina from Miami. I pity you if you think you're going to out-shout me.
Ana Navarro

We should remember that just as a positive outlook on life can promote good health, so can everyday acts of kindness.
Hillary Clinton

Embrace your vulnerabilities, accept them, and forgive yourself.
Angelica Monroy

Nothing is absolute. Everything changes, everything moves, everything revolves, everything flies and goes away.
Frida Kahlo

They mustn't know my despair, I can't let them see the wounds which they have caused, I couldn't bear their sympathy and their kind-hearted jokes, it would only make me want to scream all the more.
Anne Frank

There are years that ask questions and years that answer.
Zora Neale Hurston

The bad news is that you never completely get over the loss of your beloved. But this is also the good news. They live forever in your broken heart that doesn't seal back up. And you come through. It's like having a broken leg that never heals perfectly— that still hurts when the weather gets cold, but you learn to dance with the limp.
Anne Lamott

One tiny flame could make so many other flames; one tiny flame could set afire a whole world.
Anne Rice

It's important to know your history, but most important, that you don't forget where we came from.
Bamby Salcedo

Self-care equals success. You're going to be more successful if you take care of yourself and you're healthy.
Beth Behrs

Ten long trips around the sun since I last saw that smile, but only joy and thankfulness that on a tiny world in the vastness, for a couple of moments in the immensity of time, we were one.
Ann Druyan

Only when diverse perspectives are included, respected, and valued can we start to get a full picture of the world.
Brené Brown

Great leadership isn't about control. It's about empowering people.
Brigette Hyacinth

People get to choose the type of relationship they want: ones that bolster their egos or ones that challenge them to grow.
Carol Dweck

When you find yourself stressed, ask yourself one question: Will this matter in 5 years from now? If yes, then do something about the situation. If no, then let it go.
Catherine Pulsifer

Stress is an important dragon to slay – or at least tame – in your life.
Marilu Henner

To build a strong team you must see someone else's strength as a complement to your weakness, not a threat to your position or authority.
Christine Caine

If you don't love yourself, you can't love anybody else. And I think as women we really forget that.
Jennifer Lopez

Promise yourself today that you will savor and make the best of every moment of what lies ahead. Embracing challenge, living humbly, and dedicating your talents to a higher human purpose.
Condoleezza Rice

Our society needs women to be more numerous in decision-making positions and in entrepreneurial areas. We always have to pass a twofold test: first to prove that, though women, we are no idiots, and second, the test anybody has to pass.
Cristina Fernandez de Kirchner

Success is a great deodorant.
Elizabeth Taylor

Being your true self is the most effective formula for success there is.
Danielle LaPorte

Don't mistake politeness for lack of strength.
Sonia Sotomayor

I don't like to gamble, but if there's one thing I'm willing to bet on, it's myself.
Beyoncé

We cannot direct the wind, but we can adjust the sails.
Dolly Parton

People don't leave jobs; they leave toxic work cultures.
Dr. Amina Aitsi-Selmi

By making time for self-care, you prepare yourself to be your best so you can share your gifts with the world. Rest and self-care are so important. When you take time to replenish your spirit, it allows you to serve others from the overflow. Self-care isn't selfish. You cannot serve from an empty vessel.
Eleanor Brown

Remember always that you have not only the right to be an individual; you have an obligation to be one. You cannot make any useful contribution in life unless you do this.
Eleanor Roosevelt

The moments that define us, and test us to our core, are blessings in disguise.
Jennifer Vera

Deep grief sometimes is almost like a specific location, a coordinate on a map of time. When you are standing in that forest of sorrow, you cannot imagine that you could ever find your way to a better place. But if someone can assure you that they themselves have stood in that same place, and now have moved on, sometimes this will bring hope.
Elizabeth Gilbert

I think self-awareness is probably the most important thing towards being a champion.
Billie Jean King

There is no chance, no destiny, no fate, that can circumvent or hinder or control the firm resolve of a determined soul.
Ella Wheeler Wilcox

Face challenges, fear, and frustration by seeking out knowledge and opportunities for growth.
Fanny Mairena

The tragedy in the lives of most of us is that we go through life walking down a high-walled lane with people of our own kind, the same economic situation, the same national background and education and religious outlook. And beyond those walls, all humanity lies, unknown and unseen, and untouched by our restricted and impoverished lives.
Florence Luscomb

In case you ever foolishly forget: I am never not thinking of you.
Virginia Woolf

I am in agreement with everything my father taught me and nothing my mother taught me.
Frida Kahlo

I never thought of myself as a woman leader or Latina leader; I just thought of myself as a leader.
Geisha Williams

To receive, let go.
Lida Esperanza Garzón

My multicultural sorority taught me how to find my voice and be comfortable using it. I needed to be just as forward and direct as the women around me if I wanted my opinions and ideas to be heard.
Barbara Gonzalez

A woman who writes has power, and a woman with power is feared.
Gloria Anzaldúa

Stress is not what happens to us. It's our response TO what happens. And RESPONSE is something we can choose.
Maureen Killoran

Success is to be in peace and harmony with yourself, enjoying the moment.
Guadalupe "Pita" Betancourt

Do all the good you can, for all the people you can, in all the ways you can, as long as you can.
Hillary Clinton

Every time a tear forms in your beautiful eyes, look up to the heavens and there you will see me, smiling down from God's glorious skies.
Injete Chesoni

He who believes is strong; he who doubts is weak. Strong convictions precede great actions.
Louisa May Alcott

Getting stress out of your life takes more than prayer alone. You must take action to make changes and stop doing whatever is causing the stress. You can learn to calm down in the way you handle things.
Joyce Meyer

In the face of difficult challenges remember that these are blessings in disguise, push through them with faith.
Iris Soto

If you're serious about changing your life, you'll find a way. If you're not, you'll find an excuse.
Jen Sincero

To all those who feel different, if you are part of a group that's called 'other', a group that does not get the chance to be center stage...build your own stage and make them see you.
Beyoncé

The opposite of success is not failure...it's being stuck. You have a unique gift that's meant to be shared. When fully aligned with this everlasting GIFT, an unshakable confidence becomes REAL!
Jennifer Villarreal

Grow organically and give opportunity to other people.
Lourdes Martinez

Sometimes the biggest accomplishment in life is to find yourself.
Luisa Fernanda Cicero

Being in control of your life and having realistic expectations about your day-to-day challenges are the keys to stress management, which is perhaps the most important ingredient to living a happy, healthy and rewarding life.
Marilu Henner

Don't waste your energy trying to change opinions ... Do your thing, and don't care if they like it.
Tina Fey

Self-care should include the cold shower as well as the scented tub.
Mary Catherine Bateson

Now the first suggestion is to aim high, but be aware that even before you have reached your ultimate professional destination, if you always strive for excellence, you can and should have a substantial impact on the world in which you live.
Sandra Day O'Connor

Heroism doesn't always happen in a burst of glory. Sometimes small triumphs and large hearts change the course of history.
Mary Roach

Coach once told me that I ran like a girl and I said if he ran a little faster he could too.
Mia Hamm

As people of color, we have a potent power – and a responsibility – to change events around us, not just professionally, but spiritually and politically as well.
Michelle Herrera Mulligan

When the pure basics—what we once referred to as common etiquette—are no longer recognized, it's time for society to realize how crucial the small things are.
Nita Patel

Real change, enduring change, happens one step at a time.
Ruth Bader Ginsburg

My weapon has always been language, and I've always used it, but it has changed. Instead of shaping the words like knives now, I think they're flowers, or bridges. -
Sandra Cisneros

When I am constantly running there is no time for being. When there is no time for being there is no time for listening.
Madeleine L'Engle

I really think a champion is defined not by their wins but by how they can recover when they fall.
Serena Williams

Nothing limits intelligence more than ignorance; nothing fosters ignorance more than one's own opinions; nothing strengthens opinions more than refusing to look at reality.
Sheri S. Tepper

If a Latina falls in love with someone who is insecure, it can be a nightmare.
Sofia Vergara

Although I grew up in very modest and challenging circumstances, I consider my life to be immeasurably rich.
Sonia Sotomayor

Training your mind to be in the present moment is the number one key to making healthier choices.
Susan Albers

Think about the practice of meditation as zoning in, as opposed to spacing out.
Susie Levan

Every time we ponder a thought, act on an impulse, or dwell on a desire, we are setting in motion a cause that will have a future effect. Mindfulness enables us to choose wisely.
Tamara Levitt

Circumstances determined your past, the present is embracing you, and only you can define your future.
Teresita Marsal-Avila

Engaged employees stay for what they give, while disengaged employees stay for what they get.
Terrie Nolinske

Life is challenging but I'm always up for a challenge.
Venus Williams

Snowflakes are one of nature's most fragile things, but just look what they do when they stick together.
Verna M. Kelly

When life hands you a difficult situation where you feel undervalued and disrespected, be bold and brave enough to know your worth.
Yai Vargas

Feeling successful is essential. Set mini-goals to get to your larger goal.
Yaneth Medina

Adriana's Favorite Sayings

❖ When you ask nothing and they give everything, there it is.

❖ Always keep this phrase in mind...I want, I can, and I am able.

❖ For love you don't have to give up anything, not your friends, not your talent, not your tastes. Love adds, does not subtract

❖ When you feel that place is no longer your place...fly.

❖ Happiness also consists of what you let go, for your own good. (Coco Chanel)

❖ There's nothing bad from which good doesn't come.

❖ And it is not worth leaving this world if you have given so much pleasure to life. (Frida Kahlo)

❖ Love is born by the small details and dies from the lack of them.

❖ My family is the best gift life could give me.

❖ Of all the things you're wearing, your attitude is the most important.

❖ Make peace with your past so you don't have conflicts with your present.

❖ A real man is one who seeks a thousand ways to fall in love every day, with the same woman.

❖ To mature is to learn to want beautiful, to miss in silence, to remember without hard feelings, and to forget slowly. (Frida Kahlo)

❖ When you don't let go, you carry it. What you carry, it weighs on you. And what weights on you sinks you. Practice the art of letting go, and letting go.

❖ People think that being alone at home is loneliness. I call it absolute peace.

❖ The woman has only one defect, she does not recognize how valuable she is.

❖ The true maturity is to shut up, smile, turn around, and change paths. Because where ignorance speaks, intelligence is silent.

❖ He who leaves after a taste, a love, and a coffee does not understand how ephemeral life is.

❖ You laugh for a while with a friend and life resets you.

❖ Leaving some places is also taking care of yourself. To get away from some people is also to protect yourself. Closing some doors is also love.

❖ My dad always told me: strive, study, work because if one day you get married and a bad man touches you, you send him to hell and go ahead alone.

❖ A good relationship is based on mutual trust, shared fantasies, and an available eroticism. (Walter Riso)

❖ When you take pleasure in solitude, it is difficult to get excited again with anyone.

❖ Behind every successful woman is herself encouraging to move on.

❖ I like people who know how to be sun. Even when life is cloudy.

❖ An enterprising woman has the luxury of being with whom she wants and not with whom she touches.

❖ If you look taller with a heel, with self-love you will look immense.

❖ Sitting like Buddha, standing like Joan of Arc.

❖ The only impossible thing is what you don't try.

❖ When a woman knows where she is going, she has two options: accompany her or get out of her way.

❖ A wise man said:

> GIVE...but don't let them use it.
>
> LOVE...but don't let them abuse your heart.
>
> TRUST...but don't be naïve.
>
> LISTEN...but don't lose your own voice.

❖ Behind a happy woman, she finds herself fighting everything to keep herself that way.

❖ Make peace with your past, so it doesn't ruin your future.

❖ What others think of you is not your problem.

❖ The only person capable of making you happy is yourself.

❖ When the situation is good, enjoy it. When the situation is bad, transform it. When the situation cannot be transformed, transform yourself. (Viktor Frankl)

Acknowledgements

This book would not have been possible without the inspiration of several very important women in my life such as: my sister, friend, and confidante Amelia.

My Aunt Palle who with her discretion, family focus, and integrity have been a great example for me to follow. Martha for her love and unconditional support. My cousins Ana Paula and Ceci.

My "sisters in life" Oriana, Annie, Silvia, Kata, Carolina, María Amparo, Ileana, and María Antonieta. With each of them I carry priceless memories in my heart and wonderful and unforgettable experiences.

To my first great boss and friend Beatriz Resler and my Colombian friends and colleagues that I greatly appreciate, value, and admire: Carol, Mafe, and Ayda.

A special thanks to Héctor Castañeda for the excellent work in the design of this book cover and to my dear friend and great artist Berenice Lacroix, who created this beautiful work of art for the book.

I also want to thank a few important men who have been very meaningful to me through all my life.

First, my two fathers Arturo and Beto for their unconditional support, love, dedication, advice, and guidance in the 45 short years of my life. And to my dear brother Carlos with whom I have shared so much since childhood.

To Enrique, my best boss and unconditional friend. For over 25 years, we continue to maintain a unique and exceptional friendship.

Paco Partida, another great boss and friend, who believes in my professional potential and is a great human being.

And lastly, for the two very special men in my life. To Steven, for magically appearing in my life and changing it in a romantically different and special way. I am grateful for having you in my life. This book would not have been possible without your help and support from start to finish.

And finally, my most precious treasure, my great engine and motivation for my life, and my reason for being and existing, my son ALFONSO.

About the Author

Adriana Fuentes Díaz was born in Mexico City, spent most of her childhood and early adult years in Venezuela, and return to her city of birth seven years ago. She also lived in Newark, Delaware for a year as high school Exchange Student with a wonderful family.

After graduating with a degree in Communication and Advertising in Venezuela, Adriana studied Public Relations at McGill University in Montreal, Canada. This led to a 15-year career in marketing, communications, and public relations across a wide range of industries, including oil & gas, automotive, entertainment, beauty and skincare products, and financial services.

Passionate about branding, she is the recipient of three prestigious Advertising Industry Awards for her work on television commercials for the Mercedes-Benz brand in Mexico, including a Cannes Bronze Lion, an Ojo de Iberoamérica, and an A&AD (Global Association for Creative Advertising & Design). She also promotes her passion for branding with talks on luxury brands and marketing at the Universidad Iberoamericana in Mexico City.

While at the BBDO advertising company in Mexico City, Adriana was the leader of the BBDO Inspira program where she delivered workshops for women staff in search of personal and professional balance. In addition, she has been a volunteer and a supporter of programs and organizations of women entrepreneurs to foster gender equality in the professions and workplace.

A deeply committed dog lover for many years, Adriana created Gente Zoo, a foundation in Venezuela for stray animals on the streets, which is supported by a wide range of professionals.

Besides her devotion to her teenage son, her hobbies include traveling, reading, exercising outdoors, and sharing meals with family and friends.

www.ingramcontent.com/pod-product-compliance
Lightning Source LLC
Chambersburg PA
CBHW021011090426

42738CB00007B/743